UI State Management

From Object-Oriented to Functional

UI State Management

From Object-Oriented to Functional

Cristian Salcescu

ISBN-13: 979-8711726913

History:

March 2021 First Edition

UI State Management

From Object-Oriented to Functional

Cristian Salcescu

Contents

6

8

Introduction

Nowadays state management has become a common challenge when developing web applications. The time when we directly changed the UI for display data is long gone. All major UI libraries come with a new approach, changing the UI means actually changing the state.

The obvious question now is what state actually is.

State is data basically.
Is any data used in the application state?
The answer is "No". Only the data that is stored becomes state. If the data doesn't change then is just a configuration object used inside the application. If the data is taken from the API and then displayed on the screen without being stored we are dealing with data transfer objects.

Modifying the state in order to update UI, instead of changing directly the screen, simplifies the task of rendering the UI.

Consider for example the operation of displaying a list of notes. Presenting the list means changing the UI. In order to show the list on the screen we update the state with the new list, then the UI framework recognizes the change and updates the UI.

Detecting the state changes is done in two different ways by the current UI libraries. Some of them like Svelte and Vue uses "reactive properties". These properties are connected to pieces of UI. When the reactive property changes the HTML template using it is re-rendered. Other libraries like React use immutable objects and detect changes by comparing the object references. When the object reference changes, the piece of UI using that object re-renders.

Is this technique of changing state instead of modifying the UI actually worth doing? It seems it does. All major libraries took this approach.

Instead of thinking in terms of changing the UI elements, we think about updating pieces of data.

For example:

- rendering a list of notes → means changing the list of notes in the state object
- rendering a list of categories → means the same thing, updating the list of categories in the state object
- selecting a category → implies changing the selected category in the state
- opening a dialog → implies updating a boolean marking if the dialog should be shown or not

This technique simplifies the thinking process. It should be easier to think about changing state than updating UI elements.

Wait a minute, is it really so easy?

It seems is not. What this technique actually does is to move the task of changing the UI to changing data. Maybe updating data is easier to think about but the complexity is still there.

Different libraries attempt to handle the complexity in these data changes using distinct solutions all of them trying to make things easier to do.

In this book, we are going to look at four solutions for state management. We start from options taking an object-oriented approach, then move to solutions taking a functional approach, and in the end arrive at a solution using only pure functions.

Enjoy the learning journey!

Source Code

The project files from this book are available at https://github.com/cristi-salcescu/ui-state-management.

Feedback

I will be glad to hear your feedback. For comments, questions, or suggestions regarding this book send me an email to cristisalcescu@gmail.com. Thanks in advance for considering to write a review of the book.

Requirements

In order to see state management in practice, we are going to create a note-taking application that allows us to add, edit, delete notes, and organize them into categories.

The board displays all notes for the selected category.

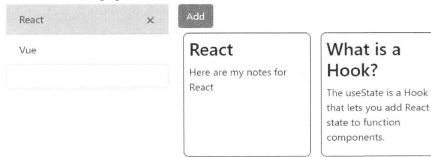

Pressing the add button on the board opens a dialog for creating a new note.

The same dialog is used for editing an existing note. From here the user can also delete the note.

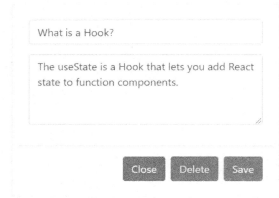

The left menu allows the user to add a new category or to delete the existing ones. The category should be selected before being deleted.

Fake API

In order to build the application, we need an API that supports the required functionalities. We can simply create a fake API using JSON Server.

Start by installing the JSON Server.

```
npm install -g json-server
```

Then create a simple JSON file with two empty lists of categories and notes. Here is the db.json file:

```
{
  "categories": [],
  "notes": []
}
```

In the end, start JSON Server.

```
json-server --watch db.json -p 3001
```

Now the following APIs are available.

```
http://localhost:3001/categories
http://localhost:3001/notes
```

Category API

The category API permits to read, create, or delete categories.

```
GET     /categorie
POST    /categories
DELETE  /categories/1
```

Here is an example of a few categories.

```
{
  "categories": [
    {
      "id" : 1,
      "name" : "React"
    },
    {
      "id" : 2,
      "name" : "Vue"
    }
  ]
}
```

Notes API

The notes API permits to create, read, update, and delete notes.

```
POST    /notes
GET     /notes
PUT     /notes/1
DELETE  /notes/1
```

Below is a sample of a few notes.

```
{
  "notes": [
    {
      "id" : 1,
      "title" : "React",
      "content" : "Here are my notes for React",
      "categoryID" : 1
    },
    {
      "id" : 2,
      "title" : "Vue",
      "content" : "Here are my notes for Vue",
      "categoryID" : 2
    }
  ]
}
```

Now that we know the requirements and have started the fake API we can begin building the application.

Chapter 01: Models and Views

Separating data from its visual representation may be an obvious thing to do now but it wasn't so from the very beginning.

Backbone was one of the first libraries to focus on this separation. It proposed a simple idea, to keep data in models and render that data using views.

The model stores and manages the data. It loads and saves that data from the backend. It emits events when that data changes.

The view listens for data changes and renders the data in the UI. It listens for the user iteration and sends the input data to the model. A view is just a part of the user interface.

Models

Models are objects managing data.

In the Backbone terminology, a model refers to a single item and a collection indicates a list of models.

Model collections have methods for changing and reading data.

Changing Data

Let's look at a few methods available on a model collection to see how data management is done.

`add(models)` adds a model or an array of models to the collection. It fires an `add` event for each model and an `update` event afterward.

```
model.add({title: "My note"});
```

remove(models) removes a model or an array of models from the collection. It fires a remove event for each model, and a single update event afterward.

reset([models]) replaces a collection with a new list of models triggering a single reset event afterward.

Reading Data

where(attributes) returns an array of all the models in a collection matching a filter object.

fetch() fetches the models from the server and then sets the result on the collection. It delegates to Backbone.sync.

Backbone.sync

Backbone has a pre-configured way to connect to a RESTful API. All the backend modifications are delegated to the Backbone.sync internal object.

The default sync handler maps CRUD operations to REST APIs like this:

- Create → POST /collection
- Read → GET /collection[/id]
- Update → PUT /collection/id
- Delete → DELETE /collection/id

Events

Models fire standard events like add, remove, change, reset, but can also trigger custom events using the trigger() method.

Views

Views are objects rendering data. They have a render() method that generates the HTML for the model data and displays it on screen. Backbone is agnostic in the way the HTML is generated.

The main idea is to split the UI into small views and have these views subscribing to model changes. When a model changes only the views listening to its changes will redraw.

Listening to Events

Views listen for model events and render the UI.

on(event, callback) subscribes to an event.

```
model.on("change", function(data) {
  console.log("change");
});
```

off([event], [callback]) unsubscribes from an event. The next example removes all **change** callbacks.

```
model.off("change");
```

Here is how this architecture looks like.

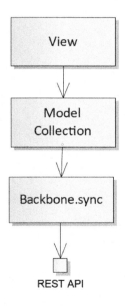

The view uses the model collection to retrieve and change data. The model collection connects to the backend API using the Backbone.sync predefined system.

Recap

The Backbone library is long gone now but its core ideas may be relevant even today.

Models store and manage data.

Views translate the data into a visual HTML interface.

This kind of separation is easy to understand and follow. The only downside is that it tends to be hard to manage when the application starts to have many-to-many relations between views and models. In that case, changing data in a model affects multiple views, and a view can make changes in several models. As long as there is a one-to-one relation between models and views, this separation is a simple and good pattern to follow.

Chapter 02:
Object-Oriented State
Management with Svelte

We will start looking at state management from an object-oriented perspective. This implies, of course, splitting responsibilities between objects.

There are two kinds of objects in an application, data and behavior objects. The common behavior object used for managing state data is the store.

Let's find out what kind of state data we can find in an application and how we can split the responsibilities of managing it between stores.

Data Objects

Data objects are used to structure and transfer data inside the application. A data object is not necessarily state. It becomes state once is stored.

Here is an example of a note data object:

```
{
  id : 1,
  title : "React",
  content : "Here are my notes for React",
  categoryID : 1
}
```

Below is a simple category data object:

```
{
  id : 2,
  name : "Vue"
```

}

State

State is stored data that changes.

The state data may come from the server, from the UI or it is necessary to support the UI functionality. As such we can identify two kinds of state data in an application: domain state and UI state.

The state data is transferred around the application. It moves between layers and between components.

Domain State

The data got from the server and stored becomes domain state.

In the case of our simple application of managing notes, the server offers two APIs one for managing notes and another one for handling categories. Both notes and categories are part of the domain state.

UI State

The UI state is needed to support user interaction. It can be created from the user input or it can be necessary to support specific interface functionality. The common example of displaying and hiding a dialog requires a boolean state property.

In the application managing notes, the user is able to select a category, select a note, open the note dialog for adding or editing.

The UI state, in this case, is made of:

- the selected category
- the selected note
- a boolean indicating if the note dialog should be shown

Stores

A store is an object that stores the state.

In our application, we split responsibilities for managing notes and categories between the `NoteStore` and the `CategoryStore`.

When reading notes we use the `NoteStore`. When modifying a note again we use the `NoteStore`.

Each store is a single source of truth for the associated state. When we need to read or modify a specific state we use the store object managing that data. It notifies subscribers when its state changes.

The domain store keeps and manages the domain state.

The UI store keeps the state related to UI. It is a simple store with not too much logic in it. It is a good idea to have one UI store per page.

Layers

A common way to split responsibilities in an application is to separate them into the three principal layers:

- UI (aka Presentation)
- Business
- Data Access

This makes it easier to understand the layer's purpose and also by moving the logic out of the UI layer it becomes easier to test.

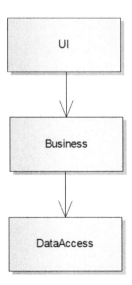

Stores in Svelte

Svelte provides a set of functions for creating readable, writable, and derived stores.

Svelte stores are reactive. Any store that correctly implements the `subscribe` method is a valid reactive store.

Here is an example of using `writable` function to create a store. It returns an object with the `subscribe`, `set` and `update` methods.

```
import { writable } from 'svelte/store';

const countStore = writable(0);

countStore.subscribe(value => {
console.log(value);
});
//0
countStore.set(1);
//1

countStore.update(n => n + 1);
//2
```

As the name says, `countStore`, is a reactive store managing a simple counter.

`set` takes the new value as an argument and updates the state with the new one.

`update` takes a callback as the first argument and uses it to compute a new value and update the state. The callback is a function taking the existing state value as its argument and returning the new value.

Recap

State is data that is stored and can be changed.

The stored data can be made of primitives and plain data objects. Data objects transfer the data around the application.

Stores are things with responsibilities. They encapsulate the state and offer a small public interface to work with that state. Stores created with Svelte helper functions are reactive.

Domain stores manage data from backend API.

UI stores keep UI-related data for facilitating user interactions.

Our natural way of dealing with complexity is to break it into smaller pieces. Objects are a way to split the responsibilities of the system into smaller parts.

Chapter 03: State Management in Practice with Svelte

In this chapter, we are going to identify all the necessary objects inside the note-taking application and define their responsibilities.

Start by creating a Svelte project.

```
npx degit sveltejs/template notes-app
```

APIs

The API objects handle the network communication.

Category API

The category API object is responsible for communicating with the external REST API to access the category related backend data. All its public methods return promises.

A promise is an object that gives access to a future result of an asynchronous operation like fetching data from a backend API.

Axios is an easy to use promise-based library used to make HTTP requests.

`fetchCategories` retrieves all the categories.

```
import axios from 'axios';
const baseUrl = 'http://localhost:3001';

function fetchCategories(){
  return axios
```

```
    .get(`${baseUrl}/categories`)
    .then(getData);
}

function getData(response){
  return response.data;
}
```

Promises are chainable using the **then** method.

The **getData** function, extracting out the **data** property from the result, is used to transform the network result using chaining. The returned value of the **fetchCategories** function is a promise giving access to the **data** property of the response object.

addCategory makes an API call to add a new category.

```
function addCategory(data){
  return axios
    .post(`${baseUrl}/categories`, data)
    .then(getData);
}
```

deleteCategory does a network call to delete a category by id.

```
function deleteCategory(id){
  return axios
    .delete(`${baseUrl}/categories/${id}`)
    .then(getData);
}
```

The category API object is exported to be used by other modules.

```
const api = {
  fetchCategories,
  addCategory,
  deleteCategory
}

export default api;
```

Note API

The notes API object handles the network requests for accessing the notes backed data.

`fetchNotes` gets all notes.

```
import axios from 'axios';
const baseUrl = 'http://localhost:3001';

function fetchNotes(){
  return axios.get(`${baseUrl}/notes`)
    .then(getData);
}


function getData(response){
  return response.data;
}
```

`addNote` makes the API call for adding a new note.

```
function addNote(data){
  return axios.post(`${baseUrl}/notes`, data)
    .then(getData);
}
```

`editNote` does the network call for updating an existing note with a new one.

```
function editNote(data){
  return axios.put(`${baseUrl}/notes/${data.id}`, data)
    .then(getData)
}
```

`deleteNote` makes the API call for deleting an existing note by id.

```
function deleteNote(id){
  return axios.delete(`${baseUrl}/notes/${id}`)
    .then(getData)
}
```

A single instance of the notes API object is created and exported.

```
const api = {
  fetchNotes,
  addNote,
  editNote,
  deleteNote
};
```

```
export default api;
```

Stores

Stores manage the domain and UI state. We are going to split the state management responsibility between several stores.

`CategoryStore` and `NoteStore` are the domain stores.

`UIStore` is the store managing the UI related state.

Category Store

The `CategoryStore` manages the list of categories.

```
import { writable } from 'svelte/store';
import api from '../api/category';

function CategoryStore() {
  const { subscribe, set, update } = writable([]);

  function loadCategories(){
    return api
      .fetchCategories()
      .then(set);
  }

  function addCategory(name){
    const category = {name}
    return api
      .addCategory(category)
      .then(loadCategories)
  }

  function deleteCategory(id){
    return api
      .deleteCategory(id)
      .then(loadCategories)
  }

  return {
    subscribe,
```

```
    loadCategories,
    addCategory,
    deleteCategory
  };
}
```

```
const store = CategoryStore();
```

```
export default store;
```

The store encapsulates the list of categories. Components can access this list by subscribing to the store using the `subscribe` method.

`loadCategories` makes an API call to retrieve all the categories, then updates the state.

`addCategory` makes the network call to add the new category and then calls `loadCategories` to refresh the state.

`deleteCategory` makes the network call to delete a category and then calls `loadCategories` to refresh the state.

The `CategoryStore` function creating the store is a factory function.

A single store is created and exported. The state is encapsulated inside this object. It can be accessed only using its methods.

```
const store = CategoryStore();
```

```
export default store;
```

Note Store

The `NoteStore` manages the list of notes.

```
import { writable } from 'svelte/store';
import api from '../api/note';

function NoteStore() {
  const { subscribe, set, update } = writable([]);

  function loadNotes(){
    return api.fetchNotes()
      .then(notes => set(notes))
  }
```

```
function saveNote(note){
  return note.id
    ? editNote(note)
    : addNote(note);
}

function addNote(note){
  return api.addNote(note)
    .then(loadNotes)
}

function editNote(note){
  return api.editNote(note)
    .then(loadNotes)
}

function deleteNote(id){
  return api.deleteNote(id)
    .then(loadNotes)
}

return {
  subscribe,
  loadNotes,
  saveNote,
  deleteNote
};
}

const store = NoteStore();

export default store;
```

loadNotes use the API object to make the network call to get all notes, then updates the state.

addNote makes the network call to add a new note and then reloads all notes by calling the loadNotes function.

The editNote and deleteNote methods update and delete a note in a similar way.

A single store is created and exported.

UI Store

The UI store handles the UI related state.

```
import { writable } from 'svelte/store';

const emptyNote = {
  title : '',
  content : ''
};

function UIStore() {
  const { subscribe, set, update } = writable({
    selectedCategory: {},
    selectedNote: emptyNote,
    isNoteEditDialogVisible: false
  });

  function selectCategory(selectedCategory){
    update(state => ({
      ...state,
      selectedCategory
    }));
  }

  function selectNote(note){
    update(state => ({
      ...state,
      selectedNote : note,
      isNoteEditDialogVisible : true
    }));
  }

  function openCreateNote(){
    update(state => ({
      ...state,
      selectedNote : emptyNote,
      isNoteEditDialogVisible : true
    }));
```

```
  }

  function closeCreateNote(){
    update(state => ({
      ...state,
      isNoteEditDialogVisible : false
    }));
  }

  return {
    subscribe,
    selectCategory,
    selectNote,
    openCreateNote,
    closeCreateNote
  };
}

const store = UIStore();

export default store;
```

`selectCategory` updates the selected category.

`selectNote` marks the note dialog to be shown and sets the selected note to the new one.

`openCreateNote` marks the note dialog to be shown and sets the selected note to an empty one.

`closeCreateNote` marks the note dialog to be hidden.

Derived Stores

The derived stores offer an option for managing a computed state.

`filteredNotes` is a derived store computing a new list based on state from the `ui` and `notes` stores.

```
import notes from './note.js';
import ui from './ui.js';
import { derived } from 'svelte/store';

export default derived(
```

```
  [notes, ui],
  ([$notes, $ui]) => {
    return filterByCategory($notes, $ui.selectedCategory);
  }, []);
```

```
function filterByCategory(){}
function isInCategory(){}
```

The `filteredNotes` returns the filtered list of notes. It reads all the notes from the `notes` store and the selected category from `ui` and uses the `filterByCategory` function to compute the result.

The derived utility function creates a store whose value is based on values from one or more other stores. The first argument defines the store's dependencies. The second argument, the callback function, computes the new value and runs whenever those dependencies change. The third argument is the initial computed value before the callback is first called.

`isInCategory` takes a category and returns a function taking a note and checking if the note is in that category.

```
function isInCategory(category){
  return function(note){
    return note.categoryID === category.id;
  }
}
```

`isInCategory` is a curried function.

A curried function is a function that takes several arguments one at a time. Given a function with two arguments, it takes one argument and returns a function taking the remaining argument. The last function returns the result using all the arguments.

`filterByCategory` gets a list of notes and a category and returns only the notes in that category.

```
function filterByCategory(notes, category){
  return notes.filter(isInCategory(category));
}
```

Recap

The `writable` helper function in Svelte can be used to create domain and UI stores.

The state management for the note-taking application can be split between two domain stores, `NoteStore` and `CategoryStore`, and a single `UIStore`. These stores are reactive and components can access the state data by listening for changes using the `subscribe` method.

The derived store available in Svelte using the `derived` helper function can help us retrieving computed state from several stores.

Chapter 04: UI in Practice with Svelte

All modern UI libraries have a component-based approach. The screen is split into these smaller parts called components and then combine together to create the original page.

App Component

We are going to divide the page into three parts that are then joined together in the **App** root component.

```
<div class="container">
  <h1>Notes Application</h1>
  <div class="row">
    <div class="col-3">
      <CategoryList />
      <NewCategory />
    </div>
    <div class="col-9">
      <Board />
    </div>
  </div>
</div>

<script>
import CategoryList from './CategoryList.svelte';
import NewCategory from './NewCategory.svelte';
import Board from './Board.svelte';
</script>
```

A component in Svelete has three parts, the template, the logic, and the style section. The logic accessing data from the store and handling user interaction stays inside the `<script>` element.

Components are organized in a tree-like structure. Here is how it looks at this point.

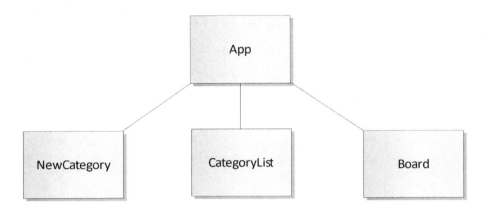

Board Component

The `Board` component displays the list of the selected notes and allows us to open the create note dialog.

```
<div>
  <div class="row">
    <button
      type="button"
      class="btn btn-primary"
      on:click={ui.openCreateNote} >
      Add
    </button>
  </div>
  <EditNote />
  <div class="row">
    {#each $filteredNotes as note}
      <Note note={note} />
    {/each}
  </div>
</div>
```

```
<script>
import EditNote from './EditNote.svelte';
import Note from './Note.svelte';

import notes from './stores/note.js';
import ui from './stores/ui.js';
import filteredNotes from './stores/filteredNotes';

notes.loadNotes();
</script>
```

The Board component accesses the note store and calls the loadNotes action method fetching all the notes.

The selected list of notes are read from the filteredNotes store and then used in the template.

```
<div class="row">
  {#each $filteredNotes as note}
    <Note note={note} />
  {/each}
</div>
```

The each block is used to iterate over the collection of notes and create the HTML for each note using the Note component.

The ui store is accessed and then used to handle the click event on the add button by calling the openCreateNote method.

```
<button
 type="button"
 on:click={ui.openCreateNote} >
   Add
</button>
```

Note that the Board component uses the other two components, Note and EditNote. Here is the updated tree of components.

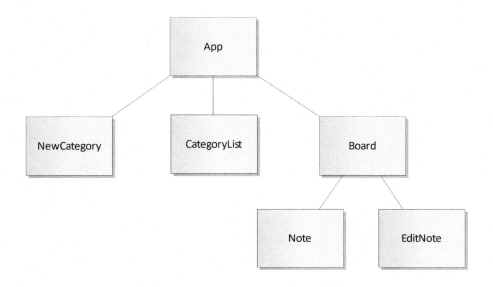

Note Component

The Note component displays a single note on the board. It gets the note data object as input.

```
<div
 class="note"
 on:click={ui.selectNote(note)} >
    <h3>{note.title}</h3>
    <div>{note.content}</div>
</div>

<script>
import ui from './stores/ui';

export let note;
</script>

<style>
.note {}
</style>
```

The note data object is sent by the parent Board component. It is not taken from the store.

The `ui` store is used to handle the click event on the note element by calling the `selectNote` method.

```
<div on:click={ui.selectNote(note)}>
</div>
```

Category List Component

The `CategotyList` component displays the list of categories.

```
<ul class="list-group">
  {#each $categories as { id, name }}
  {#if $ui.selectedCategory.id === id}
  <li
   on:click={ui.selectCategory({ id })}
   class="list-group-item" >
     <span>{name}</span>
     <button
      type="button"
      class="close"
      on:click={categories.deleteCategory(id)}>
        <span aria-hidden="true">
          &times;
        </span>
      </button>
    </li>
    {:else}
    <li
     on:click={ui.selectCategory({ id })}
     class="list-group-item">
       <span>{name}</span>
    </li>
  {/if}
 {/each}
</ul>

<script>
import categories from './stores/categories.js';
import ui from './stores/ui.js';

categories.loadCategories();
</script>
```

The component accesses the `categories` store and calls `loadCategories` for loading all the categories that are then used in the template.

It uses the each block to render all the categories and the conditional rendering to show the selected category with a different background color. It requires access to the `ui` store to read the selected category.

Edit Note Component

The `EditNote` component displays a dialog that allows adding or editing a note.

```
{#if $ui.isNoteEditDialogVisible}
<div
 class="overlay"
 v-show="show">
   <form class="dialog">
     <div class="modal-body">
     <div class="form-group">
       <input
        type="text"
        bind:value={title}
        class="form-control"
       />
       </div>
       <div class="form-group">
       <textarea
        rows="4"
        bind:value={content}
        class="form-control" />
       </div>
       </div>
       <div class="modal-footer">
       <button
        type="button"
        class="btn btn-secondary"
        on:click={ui.closeCreateNote}>
          Close
       </button>
       <button
        type="button"
        class="btn btn-danger"
```

```
        on:click={deleteNote}>
            Delete
        </button>
        <button
         type="button"
         class="btn btn-primary"
         on:click={saveNote} >
            Save
        </button>
      </div>
  </form>
</div>
{/if}

<script>
import ui from './stores/ui';
import notes from './stores/note';

let  title = '';
let  content = '';

function createNote(){
  return {
    ...$ui.selectedNote,
    title: title,
    content: content,
    categoryID : $ui.selectedCategory.id
  };
}

function deleteNote(){
  notes.deleteNote($ui.selectedNote.id);
  ui.closeCreateNote();
}

function saveNote(){
  const note = createNote();
  notes.saveNote(note);
  ui.closeCreateNote();
}
```

```
ui.subscribe(state => {
  title = state.selectedNote.title;
  content = state.selectedNote.content;
});
</script>
```

The component needs access to the `ui` store in order to decide if the dialog should be displayed based on the `isNoteEditDialogVisible` property. It accesses the `note` store to save or delete a note.

The component has an internal state.

```
let  title = '';
let  content = '';
```

This state is associated with two input fields. When the state changes, the values in the associated inputs change. When the input text changes, the state is also updated.

```
<form class="dialog">
  <input
   type="text"
   bind:value={title}
  />
  <textarea
   bind:value={content}
  />
</form>
```

Because the state is split between several stores, the component has to coordinate updates in multiple stores. For example, `saveNote()` saves the note in the notes store then closes the dialog using the `ui` store. `deleteNote()` does a similar thing.

New Category Component

The `NewCategory` component renders a form for adding a new category.

```
<form>
  <div class="form-group">
  <input
   type="text"
   class="form-control"
```

```
  bind:value={title}
 />
 </div>
 {#if title !== ''}
 <div>
   <button
    type="button"
    class="btn btn-primary"
    on:click={addCategoryAndClear}>
      Add
    </button>
 </div>
 {/if}
</form>

<script>
import categories from './stores/categories';

let title= '';

function addCategoryAndClear(){
  categories.addCategory(title);
  title = '';
}
</script>
```

The component has a local state associated with the text field.

```
let title= '';
```

The `title` local state is displayed in the input text. When the input text changes the `title` state changes.

```
<input
 type="text"
 bind:value={title}
/>
```

It uses conditional rendering to show the add button only when the associated text field is not empty.

```
{#if title !== ''}
  <div>
```

```
  </div>
{/if}
```

Entry Point

In the application entry point, the `main.js`, the `App` root component is created and rendered.

```
import App from './App.svelte';
import 'bootstrap/dist/css/bootstrap.css';

const app = new App({
 target: document.body,
 props: {
  name: 'world'
 }
});

export default app;
```

Recap

Libraries like Svelte, Vue or React display state. They turn the state into HTML and CSS.

In a composed-based design, we split the page into small components and create a tree-like structure.

Form components have a local state.

Components access stores to read the state data and call methods modifying that state. Data moves in the components' tree from parent to child using properties.

Chapter 05: Introduction to Vuex

Vuex is a centralized store that enables a unidirectional data flow inside a Vue application.

In this flow, all components connect to the store and read the data. Components dispatch actions on user interactions. Actions coordinate asynchronous operations and commit mutations. Mutations change the state. Once the state is changed the components using that state rerenders.

The Vuex pattern implies:

- The state is centralized in the store.
- The state can be changed by committing mutations, which are synchronous transactions.
- Asynchronous operations are done using actions.

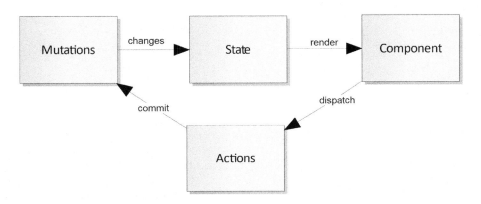

Let's look at the main parts of this state management pattern.

Store

The Vuex store keeps and manages all the application state. There is only one such store.

State

The Vuex store handles a single state object containing all the application data that can change. This way the state can be easily located and accessible from everywhere.

Getters

Getters are functions that get the whole state as input and return a computed value or part of the state. The getter's result is cached based on its dependencies and is recomputed only when dependencies have changed.

Mutations

Mutations are the only place where the state changes.

Mutations are functions that receive the state as the first argument and perform the actual state modifications.

Mutation can be called using the `store.commit()` method and passing the mutation name at the first argument. We can send an additional payload argument to the commit method as the second argument.

Mutation functions must be synchronous. We can think of them as synchronous transactions.

Actions

Actions commit mutations.

Actions can contain asynchronous operations.

Actions are dispatched using the `context.dispatch` method.

Action functions get the context object as the first parameter. It gives them access to the `context.commit` for committing a mutation, and to the state and getters via `context.state` and `context.getters`.

Modules

The Vuex store can be divided into modules. Each module contains its own state, mutations, actions, and getters.

When the store becomes big we can start splitting the actions, mutations, and getters into separate files.

Recap

The Vuex data flow is unidirectional. The store holds all application state. Components render the state and dispatch actions in response to user interactions. Actions perform custom-specific logic and invoke mutations changing the state.

The Vuex store is reactive. When the store's state changes the components using that state are updated. The only way to change the store's state is by committing mutations.

The advantage of this pattern comes when we have several components reading the same state or dispatching the same actions.

The state, getters, mutations, and actions can be split into sub-modules.

Chapter 06: State Management in Practice with Vuex

The Vuex store takes a slightly different approach. Instead of having several stores managing part of the state, Vuex offers a single store with several modules. This kind of approach enables us to access the state from other modules inside the current one.

Store

We are going to split the store into two modules, `category` and `note`, each handling a specific part of the state.

```
import { createStore } from 'vuex';

import category from './modules/category';
import note from './modules/note';

const store = createStore({
  modules: {
    category,
    note
  }
})

export default store;
```

Category Module

The category module manages all categories.

State

We need to display the list of categories on the screen. That means storing this list first. We have to mark the selected category with a specific color, which implies saving the selected category.

```
const state = {
  categories: [],
  selectedCategory: {},
};
```

Getters

Two getters are required to retrieve all the categories and the selected category from the store.

```
const getters = {
  categories(state){
    return state.categories;
  },
  selectedCategory(state){
    return state.selectedCategory;
  }
};
```

Getters take the module state as the first input and return part of that state or a newly computed value.

Mutations

We need mutations to change the state data.

```
const mutations = {
  setCategories(state, categories) {
    state.categories = categories;
    state.selectedCategory = categories[0];
  },
  selectCategory(state, category) {
    state.selectedCategory  = category;
  }
```

```
};
```

Mutations take the current state as the first parameter and the new value as the second parameter.

`setCategories` updates the current list of categories and sets the first category as the selected category.

`selectCategory` updates the selected category.

Actions

All the communications with the external backend APIs are coordinated inside actions.

```
import api from '../../api/category';

const actions = {
  loadCategories(){},
  addCategory(){},
  deleteCategory(){}
}
```

Actions take the context object as the first parameter and the new value as the second input. The `dispatch` and `commit` methods are available on the context object.

The `loadCategories` action makes a network request using the API utility function and then updates the state by committing the `setCategories` mutation.

```
loadCategories({ commit }){
  return api
    .fetchCategories()
    .then(categories => commit('setCategories', categories));
},
```

The `addCategory` action makes an API request to add the new category, then refreshes the state by dispatching the `loadCategories` action. As you can see actions can dispatch other actions and so reusing existing logic.

```
addCategory({ dispatch }, name){
  const category = {name}
    return api
```

```
    .addCategory(category)
    .then(() => dispatch('loadCategories'))
},
```

The `deleteCategory` action does a network call to delete the category and refreshes the state by dispatching the `loadCategories` action.

```
deleteCategory({ dispatch }, id){
  return api
    .deleteCategory(id)
    .then(() => dispatch('loadCategories'))
},
```

All the state, getters, mutations, and actions are exported from the category module.

```
export default {
  state,
  getters,
  mutations,
  actions
}
```

Note Module

The `note` module manages all the notes.

State

Notes need to be displayed on the screen so we have to store them first. We want to know the selected note so a state property is required for that. Showing or hiding the note dialog necessitates a boolean state value.

```
const emptyNote = {
  title : '',
  content : ''
};

const state = {
  notes: [],
  selectedNote: emptyNote,
  isNoteEditDialogVisible: false
};
```

Getters

We need getters to retrieve all the previously stored values.

```
const getters = {
  notes(state, getters, rootState, rootGetters) {
    return filterByCategory(
      state.notes,
      rootState.category.selectedCategory);
  },
  selectedNote(state){
    return state.selectedNote;
  },
  isNoteEditDialogVisible(state){
    return state.isNoteEditDialogVisible;
  }
};
```

The `notes` state stores all the notes, but the getter will retrieve only the notes from the selected category. The getter from one module can access the state and getters from other modules using `rootState` and `rootGetters`.

The `rootState.category.selectedCategory` gives access to the `selectedCategory` from the category module.

The `filterByCategory` function, used by the getter, is a pure function that gets all the notes and a category and returns a list with the notes only from that category.

```
function filterByCategory(notes, category){
  return notes.filter(isInCategory(category));
}

function isInCategory(category){
  return function(note){
    return note.categoryID === category.id;
  }
}
```

Mutations

Mutations allow changing the state in the category module.

```
const mutations = {

selectNote(){},
  openCreateNote(){},
  closeCreateNote(){},
  addNote(){},
  editNote(){},
  deleteNote(){}
};
```

The setNotes mutation updates the current list of notes with a new list.

```
setNotes(state, notes){
  state.notes = notes;
},
```

selectNote changes the selected note and also marks the note dialog to be shown.

```
selectNote(state, note){
  state.selectedNote = note;
  state.isNoteEditDialogVisible = true;
},
```

openCreateNote updates the selected note and marks the note dialog to be shown.

```
openCreateNote(state){
  state.selectedNote = emptyNote;
  state.isNoteEditDialogVisible = true;
},
```

closeCreateNote marks the edit note dialog to be hidden.

```
closeCreateNote(state){
  state.isNoteEditDialogVisible = false;
},
```

addNote adds a new note to the notes collection, updates the selected note to the new one, and marks the dialog to be hidden.

```
addNote(state, note){
  state.notes = [ ...state.notes, note];
  state.selectedNote = note;
  state.isNoteEditDialogVisible = false;
```

```
},
```

editNote updates the note in the collection, changes the selected note, and marks the dialog to be hidden.

```
editNote(state, note){
  state.notes = editItemInArray(state.notes, note);
  state.selectedNote = note;
  state.isNoteEditDialogVisible = false;
},
```

The editItemInArray helper function takes an array and an item and returns a new array with that item updated. It does not change the array but returns a new one.

```
function editItemInArray(arr, newItem){
  return arr.map(function(item){
    return item.id === newItem.id
      ? newItem
      : item;
  });
}
```

deleteNote deletes the note from the collection and marks the note dialog to be hidden.

```
deleteNote(state, id){
  state.notes = deleteFromArray(state.notes, id);
  state.isNoteEditDialogVisible = false;
}
```

The deleteFromArray utility function takes an array of items and an id and returns a new array with the item matching that id removed from it.

```
function deleteFromArray(arr, id){
  return arr.filter(note => note.id !== id);
}
```

Actions

Actions manage the API calls and then commit mutations.

```
import api from '../../api/note';

const actions = {
```

```
  loadNotes(){},
  saveNote(){},
  addNote(){},
  editNote(){},
  deleteNote(){}
};
```

loadNotes makes an API call to retrieve all the notes and then commits the setNotes to update the state with the new list.

```
loadNotes({ commit }){
  return api.fetchNotes()
    .then(notes => commit('setNotes', notes))
},
```

The addNote action makes a network call to add the new note, then commits the addNote mutation for adding the note also in the store.

```
addNote({ commit }, note){
  return api.addNote(note)
    .then(newNote => commit('addNote', newNote))
},
```

The editNote action calls the API for updating the note in the backend then commits the editNote mutation for changing the same note in the store.

```
editNote({ commit }, note){
  return api.editNote(note)
    .then(newNote => commit('editNote', newNote))
},
```

The saveNote action dispatches the editNote action when the note has an id, and the addNote when there is no such id. It can be used to autodetect editing or adding based on the id of the note.

```
saveNote({dispatch}, note){
  return note.id
    ? dispatch('editNote', note)
    : dispatch('addNote', note);
},
```

The deleteNote action makes a network call to delete the note from the backend, then commits the deleteNote mutation to delete the same note from the store.

```
deleteNote({ commit }, id){
  return api.deleteNote(id)
    .then(() => commit('deleteNote', id))
}
```

Entry Point

In the application entry point, the `main.js` file, the store is created and then used to dispatch two load actions.

```
import { createApp } from 'vue';
import App from './App.vue';
import store from './store';

createApp(App)
  .use(store)
  .mount('#app');

store.dispatch('loadCategories');
store.dispatch('loadNotes');
```

Recap

The state management task can be split between modules. Each module handles its specific part of the state.

Getters retrieve part of that state or a computed value. Getters from a module can access state or getters from other modules.

Mutations can update several state properties.

Actions orchestrate the API calls and then update the state using mutations.

Chapter 07: UI in Practice with Vue

Vue like the other UI libraries takes a component-based approach in building the interface. The page is split into small components that are then composed together.

We are going to create the same tree of components.

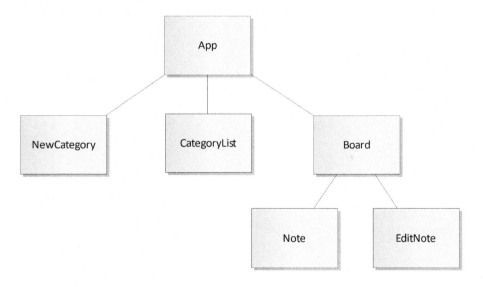

Let's look at all the necessary components one by one.

Board Component

The board displays all the current notes. Clicking on a note opens the dialog for editing it. The add button shows the same dialog for adding a new note.

```
<template>
  <div>
    <div class="row">
      <button
       type="button"
       class="btn btn-primary"
       @click="openCreateNote">
         Add
      </button>
    </div>
    <EditNote />
    <div class="row">
      <Note
       v-for="note in notes"
       :note="note"
       :key="note.id" />
    </div>
  </div>
</template>

<script>
import {
  mapGetters,
  mapMutations } from 'vuex';

import EditNote from './EditNote';
import Note from './Note';

export default {
  computed: {
    ...mapGetters([
      'notes'
    ])
  },
  methods: {
    ...mapMutations([
      'openCreateNote'
    ])
  },
```

```
  components: {
    EditNote,
    Note
  }
}
</script>
```

Similar to Svelte, a single-file Vue component puts together the template, the logic, and the styles for a piece of the user interface.

The mapGetters utility gives access to the getters in the store like the one retrieving all the current notes. Once mapped, the **notes** can be used directly in the template.

Vue uses an HTML-based template syntax that allows us to bind HTML elements to the component's data. To do that, it uses special HTML attributes prefixed with v-, called directives.

In order to transform the list of notes into **Note** component elements, Vue uses the v-for directive.

```
<Note
 v-for="note in notes"
 :note="note"
 :key="note.id" />
```

The mapMutations helper gives access to mutations in the store.

```
methods: {
  ...mapMutations([
    'openCreateNote'
  ])
},
```

The openCreateNote mutation is then used as an event handler for the add note button.

```
<button
 type="button"
 @click="openCreateNote">
  Add
</button>
```

The Board component uses two other components Note and EditNote.

Note Component

The `Note` component gets a note object and creates the user interface for it.

```
<template>
  <div
   class="note"
   @click="selectNote(note)" >
      <h3>{{note.title}}</h3>
      <div>{{note.content}}</div>
  </div>
</template>

<script>
import { mapMutations } from 'vuex';

export default {
  props : ['note'],
  methods: {
    ...mapMutations([
      'selectNote'
    ])
  }
}
</script>

<style>
.note {}
</style>
```

The `Note` component takes the input note in props. The parent component, `Board` in our case, should send the note data object to it.

The `selectNote` mutation is accessed using the `mapMutations` helper.

```
methods: {
  ...mapMutations([
    'selectNote'
  ])
}
```

When the note is clicked, the `selectNote` mutation is committed.

```
<div @click="selectNote(note)">
</div>
```

Edit Note Component

The `EditNote` component renders the note editing dialog. It is displayed only when the show property is `true`.

```
<template>
<div
 className="overlay"
 v-show="show">
  <form className="dialog">
    <div className="modal-body">
    <div className="form-group">
      <input
        type="text"
        v-model="title"
        className="form-control"
        />
    </div>
    <div className="form-group">
      <textarea
        rows="4"
        v-model="content"
        className="form-control">
        </textarea>
    </div>
    </div>
    <div className="modal-footer">
      <button
        type="button"
        className="btn btn-secondary"
        @click="closeCreateNote">
          Close
      </button>
      <button
        type="button"
        className="btn btn-danger"
        @click="deleteNote(note.id)">
         Delete
```

```
      </button>
      <button
       type="button"
       className="btn btn-primary"
       @click="saveNote(createNote())" >
         Save
      </button>
    </div>
   </form>
 </div>
</template>

<script>
import {
  mapGetters,
  mapActions,
  mapMutations } from 'vuex';

export default {
data(){
  return {
    title: '',
    content: ''
  }
},
computed: {
  ...mapGetters({
    note: 'selectedNote',
    show: 'isNoteEditDialogVisible',
    category: 'selectedCategory'
  })
},
methods: {
  ...mapActions([
    'saveNote',
    'deleteNote'
  ]),
  ...mapMutations([
    'closeCreateNote'
  ]),
```

```
  createNote(){
    return {
      ...this.note,
      title: this.title,
      content: this.content,
      categoryID : this.category.id
    };
  }
},
watch: {
  note(){
    this.title = this.note.title;
    this.content = this.note.content;
  }
 }
}
</script>

<style>
.overlay {}
.dialog {}
</style>
```

EditNote is a component with local state. Form components in general have a local state associated with their input fields.

```
data(){
  return {
    title: '',
    content: ''
  }
},
```

The local state is connected to inputs using the v-model directive. When the input changes the state is updated. When the state change the input values are updated.

```
<form>
  <input
   type="text"
   v-model="title"
   />
```

```
<textarea
 v-model="content"
</textarea>
</form>
```

The component connects to the store to access the `selectedNote` renamed as just `note`, the `isNoteEditDialogVisible` renamed as `show`, and the `selectedCategory` renamed as `category`.

All three getters are accessed using the `mapGetters` helper.

```
...mapGetters({
  note: 'selectedNote',
  show: 'isNoteEditDialogVisible',
  category: 'selectedCategory'
})
```

The `show` getter is used to display the dialog only when is `true`. This is called conditional rendering and can be done using the `v-show` directive.

```
<div v-show="show">
  <form>
  </form>
</div>
```

The `closeCreateNote` mutation is accessed using the `mapMutations` helper.

```
...mapMutations([
  'closeCreateNote'
])
```

When the close button is clicked, the `closeCreateNote` mutation is committed hiding the dialog.

```
<button
 type="button"
 @click="closeCreateNote">
   Close
</button>
```

The selected note is watched. When it changes, the local state is updated. When the local state changes the associate input values change also.

```
watch: {
  note(){
```

```
      this.title = this.note.title;
      this.content = this.note.content;
    }
  }
}
```

Category List Component

The `CategoryList` component displays the list of categories.

```
<template>
  <ul className="list-group">
  <template
   v-for="category in categories"
   :key="category.id">
    <li
     v-if="isSelectedCategory(category)"
     @click="selectCategory(category)"
     className="list-group-item" >
      <span>{{category.name}}</span>
      <button
       type="button"
       className="close"
       @click="deleteCategory(category.id)">
        <span aria-hidden="true">
          &times;
        </span>
      </button>
    </li>
    <li
     v-else
     @click="selectCategory(category)"
     className="list-group-item">
      <span>{{category.name}}</span>
    </li>
  </template>
  </ul>
</template>

<script>
import {
```

```
  mapGetters,
  mapActions,
  mapMutations } from 'vuex';

export default {
  computed: {
    ...mapGetters([
      'categories',
      'selectedCategory'
    ])
  },
  methods: {
    isSelectedCategory(category){
      return (category.id ===
        this.selectedCategory.id)
    },
    ...mapMutations([
      'selectCategory'
    ]),
    ...mapActions([
      'deleteCategory'
    ])
  }
}
</script>
```

The selected category and all the other categories are read from the store using the mapGetters helper.

```
computed: {
  ...mapGetters([
    'categories',
    'selectedCategory'
  ])
}
```

Then all the category names as displayed in a list using the v-for directive.

```
<template
 v-for="category in categories"
 :key="category.id">
 <li
```

```
    <span>{{category.name}}</span>
  </li>
</template>
```

The component uses conditional rendering to create a select button for all categories except the selected one for which a simple text is displayed.

```
<template
 v-for="category in categories"
 :key="category.id">
 <li
  v-if="isSelectedCategory(category)">
    <span>{{category.name}}</span>
    <button
     type="button">
       <span aria-hidden="true">
         &times;
       </span>
    </button>
 </li>
 <li
  v-else>
    <span>{{category.name}}</span>
 </li>
</template>
```

When the delete button is clicked, the `deleteCategory` mutation is committed.

```
<button
 type="button"
 @click="deleteCategory(category.id)">
    <span aria-hidden="true">
      &times;
    </span>
</button>
```

When the selected item is pressed, the `selectCategory` action is dispatched.

```
<li @click="selectCategory(category)">
  <span>{{category.name}}</span>
</li>
```

New Category Component

The NewCategory component creates a simple form adding a new category.

```
<template>
  <form>
    <div className="form-group">
      <input
        type="text"
        className="form-control"
        v-model="title"
      />
      </div>
      <div v-if="title !== ''" >
        <button
          type="button"
          className="btn btn-primary"
          @click="addCategoryAndClear">
            Add
        </button>
      </div>
    </form>
</template>

<script>
import { mapActions } from 'vuex';

export default {
data(){
  return {
    title: '',
  }
},
methods: {
  ...mapActions([
    'addCategory'
  ]),
  addCategoryAndClear(){
    this.addCategory(this.title);
    this.title = '';
  }
```

```
  }
}
</script>
```

As other form components, `NewCategory` has local state.

```
data(){
  return {
    title: ''
  }
},
```

The title state property is associated with an input text.

```
<input
 type="text"
 v-model="title"
/>
```

The add button is displayed only when the title input is filled. We don't need to access the input to get its value, we already have it in the state object.

```
<div v-if="title !== ''" >
  <button
   type="button">
     Add
  </button>
</div>
```

The `addCategory` action is accessed using the `mapActions` helper.

```
...mapActions([
  'addCategory'
]),
```

We want to clear the title textbox after the category is added. We need a new method that dispatches the `addCategory` actions and then clears the textbox. Changing the UI means changing the state, so clearing the textbox implies setting the associated state property to an empty string.

```
addCategoryAndClear(){
  this.addCategory(this.title);
  this.title = '';
}
```

When the add button is clicked, the custom method adding the category and clearing the textbox is called.

```
<button
 type="button"
 @click="addCategoryAndClear">
    Add
</button>
```

App Component

The App root component uses the other components to create the whole page. It does nothing more than specifying where the components should be placed on the screen.

```
<template>
  <div class="container">
    <h1>Notes Application</h1>
    <div class="row">
      <div className="col-3">
        <CategoryList />
        <NewCategory />
      </div>
      <div className="col-9">
        <Board />
      </div>
    </div>
  </div>
</template>

<script>
import CategoryList from './components/CategoryList';
import NewCategory from './components/NewCategory';
import Board from './components/Board';

export default {
  name: 'app',
  components: {
    CategoryList,
    NewCategory,
    Board
  }
```

```
}
</script>
```

Recap

Components can easily access state data from the store using the Vuex helpers.

Vuex offers a nice set of helpers for commiting mutations and dispatching actions to the store from components.

Form components usually have local state associated with their inputs.

Chapter 08: Introduction to Flux

Flux is an architectural pattern introduced by Facebook trying to address the limitations of managing data using models.

The flux architecture splits the application into the following parts:

- Stores
- Dispatcher
- Views
- Actions and action creators

Stores

Stores manage the state. They can handle both domain state and user interface state.

A store can manage several data objects. It is the single source of truth in regards to those specific data objects.

In an application, there can be many stores. In the case of the note-taking application, we can work with the `NoteStore`, the `CategoryStore`, and the `UIStore`.

Stores have methods, but these are no setter methods. Requests for state change are done by passing actions to the dispatcher.

A store listens for all actions and decides on which of them to act. This usually means a `switch` statement. Once the store has made the state changes, it will emit a change event. The store is an event emitter.

Stores don't take other stores as dependencies.

Dispatcher

A dispatcher is a single object that broadcasts actions to all registered stores. Stores need to register for listening actions when the application starts.

When an action comes in, it will pass that action to all registered stores.

Views

The view is the user interface component. It is responsible for rendering the HTML and for handling the user interaction. Views are organized in a tree-like structure.

Views listen for store changes and re-render.

Views can be further split into presentation and container Views.

Presentation views don't have access to stores or the dispatcher object. They communicate only through their own properties.

Container views are connected to stores and dispatcher. They listen for events from stores and provide the data for presentation components. They get the new data using the stores' public getter methods and then pass that data down the tree of views.

Container views dispatch actions in response to user iteration.

Actions

An action is a plain object that contains all the information necessary to do that action.

Actions have a `type` property identifying the action type.

Actions may come from different places. They may come from views as a result of user interaction. They may come from other places like the initialization code, where data may be taken from an API and actions are fired to update the views. Action may come from a timer that requires screen updates.

Action Creators

The practice is to encapsulate the code, creating actions in functions. These functions that create and dispatch actions are called action creators.

API Utils

API calls are made in action creators. We can extract out the code that does the API call in API utils functions.

When doing API calls to update the user interface, the API call will be followed by an action to update the store. When the store is updated it will emit a change event and as result, the view that listens for that event will re-render.

Unidirectional data flow

Let's start looking at the data flow for updating views.

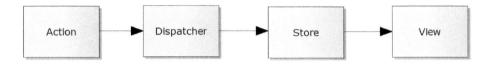

The action creator builds an action that is broadcast using the dispatcher. Stores listen for actions, update the state in response, and then emit events. Views subscribe to state change events and update the screen.

Views do not modify the data they get. However, they can create new action objects containing part of the data received.

Stores, views, and any other action can't change the state in (other) stores directly. They must send an action through the dispatcher

The data flow is shorter for reads than for writes. Views can directly access the store to read data.

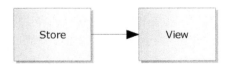

The data flow for changing the state differs between asynchronous and synchronous actions.

In order to do a state change, views build synchronous actions using actions creators that are then broadcast to the stores. Stores listen for these actions and update the state.

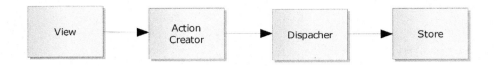

When dealing with asynchronous tasks like making an API call, views use asynchronous action creators to build actions. Asynchronous action creators can make for example API calls to retrieve data from the backend and then create and dispatch synchronous actions.

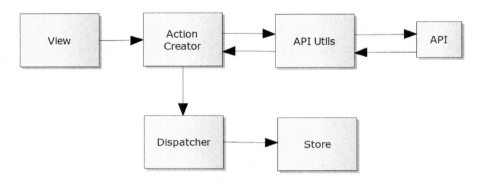

Recap

Stores manage state. They change state only by listening for actions. Stores notify views to update.

The dispatcher broadcasts actions to all registered stores.

Actions are plain objects. They can be persisted and then replayed.

Views render the user interface and handle user interaction. Views listen to store changes and update the user interface.

Data can be read directly from the stores but updates require to dispatch actions with the dispatcher.

Flux can add unnecessary complexity to an application where each view maps to one store. The Flux architecture is better in applications where views don't map directly to stores. To put it in a different way, when views can create actions that will update many stores and stores can trigger changes that will update many views.

Chapter 09: Introduction to Redux

In this chapter, we will look at state management using the Redux library.

Before discussing the architectural pattern we need to go first through a few functional principles.

Functional Programming

Functional programming is a style of programming that involves using concepts such as first-class functions, pure functions, immutability, currying or higher-order functions.

First-Class Functions

Functions are considered first-class when we can work with a function like with any other values. That means we can send a function as an argument to another function or return a function from another function. It also means functions can be stored in variables, objects properties, arrays, or any other data structures.

Immutability

An immutable object is an object that once created cannot be changed.

Primitive values are immutable, so immutability means basically treating objects also as being immutable.

Pure Functions

A pure function is a computation. It computes the result using only its input. Given a specific input, it always returns the same output.

Pure functions create and return new values based only on the input parameters.

A pure function has no side-effects. A side-effect is a change outside the function or usage of data that can change from outside the function.

Redux

The Redux architectural pattern tries to address the "dispatcher confusion" from the Flux architecture and use the functional programming principles in doing state management.

Redux unifies all the stores and the dispatcher in one object, the Redux store.

Check again the data flow in Flux. Changing the state requires dispatching an action that can go to one or more stores.

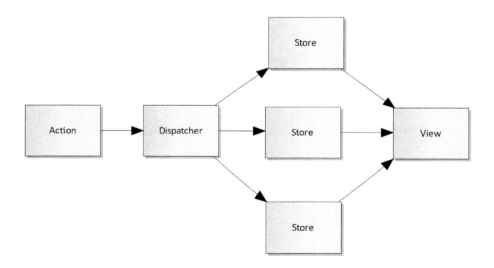

In a similar way, the action in Redux is dispatched to a single store but it can be processed by one or more reducers.

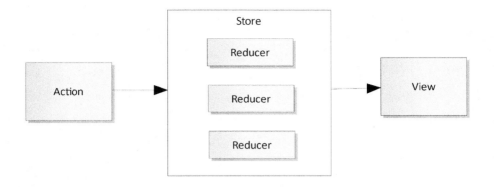

Data can be read from the store using the `getState()` method. It can then be changed by dispatching actions using the `dispatch()` method. Views can subscribe and listen for changes using the `subscribe()` method.

When we look at the Redux store it has just a few methods: `getState`, `dispatch`, `subscribe`.

The Redux store does state management following functional programming principles. That means that instead of writing functions updating the state we are going to create pure functions taking the state and an action and returning a new state object. The pure functions are called reducers and are used by the Redux store to compute the new state and then update it.

The impure logic of updating the state is done by the store. We are responsible for writing the pure logic computing new value, meaning the reducer functions.

Next, we are going to look at the main parts of the Redux pattern.

State

A state is a single object representing the entire state of an application. It can be a nested object.

Actions

Actions are plain objects describing the change that should happen in the state. They must have the `type` string property that defines the change.

Actions are dispatched at events that happen based on user interaction.

The action object can contain additional information about what happened. By convention, this extra information stays in the `payload` field.

Action Creators

Action creators are functions that return action objects. They are used to encapsulate the logic for creating the plain object.

Actions are plain objects. Action creators are functions creating those action objects.

Actions must be dispatched in order to trigger a change in the state. For that we need to call the store's `dispatch` function.

Reducers

A reducer is a function that receives the current `state` and a plain `action` object and returns the new state.

Reducers are pure functions. They do not modify the input `state` object. Updating the state means returning a new object containing the change.

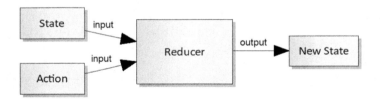

Here is how the data-flow looks at this point.

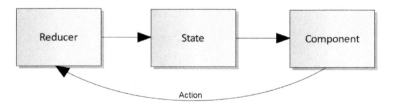

Store

All the state is managed by the Redux store.

The store is created by passing in the reducer function.

Selectors

Selectors are pure functions that take the state object as input and return part of it or a computed value

Async Action

An async action is a value representing an asynchronous operation. It can be for example a function or a promise depending on the middleware that processes it and then dispatches plain actions.

For example, an async action represented as a thunk function is intercepted by a middleware and then is executed. As a result of its execution, plain actions are dispatched.

Async Action Creators

Async action creators are functions returning async actions. For example, they may return a promise or another function.

The return function may contain side-effects like making an API call or routing the user to a different page.

Middleware

A middleware is a transformation logic that stays before the code processing the plain actions.

The middleware is useful for performing side-effects like routing or making API calls. It often turns async actions into actions.

For example, the thunk middleware intercepts thunk actions and executes them before reaching the reducer. Executing the thunk actions usually involves doing side-effects and dispatching plain actions.

Several middlewares can be added to the Redux store.

Below is the data-flow when using async actions.

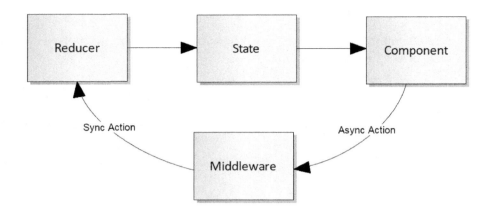

Recap

Functional programming lets us think of an application in terms of data and transformations of that data. Transforming data is done using pure functions.

Redux enables us to interact with state data using functional principles.

Reducers are pure functions that return changed copies of the current state based on the action they received as input.

Data that is computed based on other data is better calculated using a selector.

React with Redux is maybe the best option for working in a functional style at the moment in JavaScript. Redux allows managing state using pure functions and immutable data. React allows writing components using functions. We can even write those components as pure functions.

Chapter 10: State Management in Practice with Redux

In this chapter, we will look at how to manage the application state using the Redux store.

Start by building a React application using Create React App. To do that, run the following command:

```
npx create-react-app appname
```

Then install the necessary additional libraries.

```
npm install @reduxjs/toolkit --save
npm install react-redux --save
npm install axios --save
```

We are going to split the state management between two features: category and notes.

Category Feature

The category feature handles all the categories.

The state is made of a list of categories and the selected category. The root state will contain the **categories** and the **selectedCategory** branches. Each state branch will be managed by a specific reducer.

Actions

A few actions are needed for updating the list of categories, selecting a category, and creating a new category.

Action creators and types can be simply defined using the createAction helper. Instead of defining a separate action type constant and an action creator function, the `createAction` builds an action creator function that combines them.

It gets an action type and returns an action creator for that type. It also overrides the toString() of the action creator function so that it can be used as the action string type.

```
import { createAction } from '@reduxjs/toolkit';

const setCategories = createAction('setCategories');
const selectCategory = createAction('selectCategory');
const addCategory = createAction('addCategory');

export default {
  setCategories,
  selectCategory,
  addCategory
};
```

Reducers

The `selectedCategory` reducer updates the `selectedCategory` state branch with the new value when the `selectCategory` action is dispatched.

The createReducer utility function from the Redux Toolkit simplifies the creation of Redux reducer functions by mapping specific action types to smaller reducer functions. The smaller reducers update the state when that specific action is dispatched.

```
import { createReducer } from '@reduxjs/toolkit';
import actions from '../actions';

const initialState = {};

function selectCategory(state, action){
  const selectedCategory = action.payload;
  return selectedCategory;
}

export default createReducer(initialState, {
  [actions.selectCategory]: selectCategory
```

```
});
```

The `categories` reducer updates the `categories` state branch with the new list of categories when the `setCategories` action is dispatched.

```
import { createReducer } from '@reduxjs/toolkit';
import actions from '../actions';

const initialState = [];

function setCategories(state, action){
  const categories = action.payload;
  return categories;
}

export default createReducer(initialState, {
  [actions.setCategories]: setCategories
});
```

Async Action Creators / Effects

The majority of side-effects required in a practical application are encapsulated inside the asynchronous action creators. I will simply call these functions "effects" and implement them using Redux Thunk.

The `loadCategories` effect makes an API call to retrieve all the categories and then builds the `setCategories` action with the new values and dispatches it to the store.

```
import api from './api';
import actions from './actions';

function loadCategories(){
  return function(dispatch){
    return api.fetchCategories()
      .then(actions.setCategories)
      .then(dispatch)
  }
}
```

The `addCategory` effect makes an API call to add the new category and then builds and dispatches the `loadCategories` effect to the store.

Dispatching the `loadCategories` effect has the result of updating the store with the latest categories.

```
function addCategory(name){
  return function(dispatch){
    const category = {name}
    return api.addCategory(category)
      .then(loadCategories)
      .then(dispatch)
  }
}
```

The `deleteCategory` effect makes a network call to delete a category by id and then builds and dispatches the `loadCategories` effect.

```
function deleteCategory(id){
  return function(dispatch){
    return api.deleteCategory(id)
      .then(loadCategories)
      .then(dispatch)
  }
}
```

All effects are made public.

```
export default {
  loadCategories,
  addCategory,
  deleteCategory
};
```

Note Feature

The note feature manages all the notes.

The state is made of a list of notes, the selected note, and a boolean used to show the edit note dialog. The state contains the `categories` and the `noteDialog` branches. The `noteDialog` object contains the selected note and the boolean value.

Actions

Working with notes requires a few actions.

The `selectNote` is required for selecting a note and opening the edit note dialog.

The `openCreateNote` and `closeCreateNote` actions are utilized for opening and closing the note dialog.

`addNote`, `editNote`, `deleteNote` actions are used from the note dialog to add, edit, or delete notes.

```
import { createAction } from '@reduxjs/toolkit';

const setNotes = createAction('setNotes');

const selectNote = createAction('selectNote');
const openCreateNote = createAction('openCreateNote');
const closeCreateNote = createAction('closeCreateNote');

const addNote = createAction('addNote');
const editNote = createAction('editNote');
const deleteNote = createAction('deleteNote');

export default {
  setNotes,
  addNote,
  editNote,
  deleteNote,
  selectNote,
  openCreateNote,
  closeCreateNote
};
```

Reducers

The `noteDialog` reducer handles all the actions related to the note dialog.

When the `openCreateNote` action is dispatched the current note is cleared and the dialog is marked for being displayed.

When the `closeCreateNote` action is dispatched the dialog is marked for being hidden.

When the `selectNote` action is dispatched the current note is set to the new note and the dialog is marked for being displayed.

```
import { createReducer } from '@reduxjs/toolkit';
import actions from '../actions';

const emptyNote = {
  title : '',
  content : ''
};

const initialState = {
  note : emptyNote,
  show : false
};

function selectNote(state, action){
  const note = action.payload;
  return {
    ...state,
    note,
    show: true
  };
}

function openCreateNote(state, action){
  return {
    ...state,
    note: emptyNote,
    show: true
  };
}

function closeCreateNote(state, action){
  return {
    ...state,
    show: false
  }
}

export default createReducer(initialState, {
  [actions.selectNote]: selectNote,
  [actions.openCreateNote]: openCreateNote,
```

```
  [actions.closeCreateNote]: closeCreateNote
});
```

The **notes** reducer handles all the actions related to the list of notes.

When the **addNote**, **editNote**, **deleteNote** actions are triggered the specified note is added, edited, or deleted from the list.

```
import { createReducer } from '@reduxjs/toolkit';
import actions from '../actions';

const initialState = [];

function setNotes(state, action){
  const notes = action.payload;
  return notes;
}

function addNote(notes, action){
  const note = action.payload;
  return notes.concat([note]);
}

function editNote(notes, action){
  const newItem = action.payload;
  return notes.map(item => {
    return item.id === newItem.id
      ? newItem
      : item;
  });
}

function deleteNote(notes, action){
  const id = action.payload;
  return notes
    .filter(note => note.id !== id);
}

export default createReducer(initialState, {
  [actions.setNotes]: setNotes,
  [actions.addNote]: addNote,
  [actions.editNote]: editNote,
```

```
    [actions.deleteNote]: deleteNote
});
```

Notice that all small reducer functions are pure functions. They do not change the existing input state but return a changed copy.

`addNote` uses the `concat` array method to create a new array with the new value appended to the list.

`editNote` uses the `map` array method to create a new array with the note updated.

`map` transforms a list of values to another list of values using a mapping function.

`deleteNote` creates a new array with the note having the specified id deleted using the `filter` array method.

`filter` selects values from a list using a predicate function deciding what values to keep.

Selectors

Selectors retrieved part of the state or compute some derived data based on the stored information.

The `getNotes` returns only the notes that are part of the selected category. It accesses the list with all the notes and the selected category from the root state and computes the filtered list of notes.

```
function getNotes({notes, selectedCategory}){
  return notes
    .filter(isInCategory(selectedCategory));
}

function isInCategory(category){
  return function(note){
    return note.categoryID === category.id;
  }
}

export default { getNotes };
```

`isInCategory` is a curried function.

Currying is a technique of breaking down a function that takes several arguments into a series of functions that each takes only one argument.

Effects

A few effects are required from creating, reading, updating, and deleting notes from both the store and the backend API.

loadNotes makes a network call to retrieve all the notes and then dispatches the setNotes action to update the state with the new list.

```
import api from './api';
import actions from './actions';

function loadNotes(){
  return function(dispatch){
    return api.fetchNotes()
      .then(actions.setNotes)
      .then(dispatch);
  }
}
```

addNote does an API call to add a new note and then dispatches the addNote action to update the state and closes the dialog by dispatching the closeCreateNote action.

```
function addNote(note){
  return function(dispatch){
    return api.addNote(note)
      .then(actions.addNote)
      .then(dispatch)
      .then(actions.closeCreateNote)
      .then(dispatch);
  }
}
```

editNote makes a network call to update the note on the backend, then dispatches the editNote action to update the state, and in the end, dispatches the closeCreateNote action closing the edit dialog.

```
function editNote(note){
  return function(dispatch){
    return api.editNote(note)
      .then(actions.editNote)
```

```
        .then(dispatch)
        .then(actions.closeCreateNote)
        .then(dispatch);
    }
}
```

Instead of using two effect functions for adding or editing a note, we can use only one, `saveNote`, that decides which one of them to use based on the presence of the `id` in the note data object. A new note doesn't have an id.

```
function saveNote(note){
    return note.id
        ? editNote(note)
        : addNote(note);
}
```

In a similar way, the `deleteNote` effect makes an API call, then updates the state, and closes the edit dialog.

```
function deleteNote(id){
    return function(dispatch){
        return api.deleteNote(id)
            .then(() => id)
            .then(actions.deleteNote)
            .then(dispatch)
            .then(actions.closeCreateNote)
            .then(dispatch);
    }
}
```

All effects are exported.

```
export default {
    loadNotes,
    saveNote,
    editNote,
    deleteNote
};
```

Root Reducer

The root reducer handles all the actions of the application by delegating the state management to smaller reducer functions. The combineReducers utility function defines all the state branches and the associated reducer managing that state branch.

For example, the `categories` state branch is managed by the categories reducer, `selectedCategory` state branch by the `selectedCategory` reducer and so on.

```
import { combineReducers } from 'redux';
import categories from './category/reducers/categories';
import selectedCategory from
    './category/reducers/selectedCategory';
import notes from './note/reducers/notes';
import noteDialog from './note/reducers/noteDialog';

export default combineReducers({
  categories,
  selectedCategory,
  notes,
  noteDialog
});
```

Entry Point

In the application entry point, the `index.js` file, the store is created using the root reducer. When the application starts two effects are dispatched for loading all the categories and all the notes from the backend.

```
import React from 'react';
import ReactDOM from 'react-dom';
import { configureStore } from '@reduxjs/toolkit';
import { Provider } from 'react-redux';

import App from './App';
import rootReducer from './rootReducer';

import noteEffect from './note/effects';
import categoryEffects from './category/effects';

const store = configureStore({
  reducer: rootReducer
});
```

```
const rootElement = document.getElementById('root');

ReactDOM.render(
  <React.StrictMode>
  <Provider store={store}>
  <App />
  </Provider>
</React.StrictMode>, rootElement);


store.dispatch(categoryEffects.loadCategories());
store.dispatch(noteEffect.loadNotes());
```

Recap

The Redux root state can be split between branches. Each branch is managed by a specific reducer function.

The arrays methods like `filter`, `map`, `reduce`, `concat` are useful when dealing with operations creating new arrays.

The createReducer utility simplifies the building of reducer functions by mapping action types to smaller reducer functions.

Action creators can simply be built using the createAction helper.

Side-effects are mainly encapsulated inside the asynchronous actions. We implemented them as functions using Redux Thunk and simply called them "effects". Asynchronous actions can reuse and dispatch other asynchronous actions.

We can group together all actions, effects, reducers, and selectors related to a specific state branch in its own feature folder.

Chapter 11: UI in Practice with React

React, like other UI libraries, promotes a component-based design, as a result, the page is split into smaller components that are then combined to create the whole page. The difference is that components can be created using functions.

In a sense, components are function that transforms data into HTML.

Let's start defining these function components required by the note-taking application.

Board Component

The Board component takes in the list of notes and creates the HTML representation for it.

```
import React from 'react';
import { connect } from 'react-redux';

import selectors from './selectors';
import actions from './actions';
import Note from './Note';
import NoteEdit from './EditNote';

function Board({notes, openCreateNote}) {

  return (
    <div>
      <div className="row">
        <div className="col">
```

```
              <button
                type="button"
                className="btn btn-primary"
                onClick={openCreateNote}>
                    Add
              </button>
          </div>
        </div>

        <div className="row">
          {notes.map(note =>
            <Note
              note={note}
              key={note.id} />)}
        </div>

        <NoteEdit />
      </div>
    );
}
```

The component converts the list of notes into Note elements using the map array method.

```
{notes.map(note =>
    <Note note={note} key={note.id} />)
}
```

The Board component takes the openCreateNote function in props and uses it as the event handler for the open dialog click event.

```
<button
  type="button"
  onClick={openCreateNote}>
    Add
</button>
```

It connects to the store in order to read all the notes and dispatch the openCreateNote action.

```
export default connect(
  state => ({
      notes: selectors.getNotes(state)
```

```
    }), {
      ...actions
    }
  )(Board);
```

The `connect` helper function connects the component to a Redux store. It does not modify the input component but returns a new connected component. The first argument is a function that extracts the state data and maps it to the component properties. The second argument can be a map with all the actions and effects to be dispatched to the store.

A function taking another function as an argument, returning a function, or doing both is a higher-order function. `connect` is a higher-order function.

Note Component

The `Note` component creates the UI for a single note in the bord. It takes the note data object in props.

```
import React from 'react';
import { connect } from 'react-redux';

import actions from './actions';

function Note({note, selectNote}) {
  return (
    <div
      className="card col-4 m-1"
      onClick={() => selectNote(note)}>
        <div className="card-body">
          <h3 className="card-title">
            {note.title}
          </h3>
          <div className="card-text">
            {note.content}
          </div>
        </div>
    </div>
  );
}
```

The component needs to connect to the store to dispatch the `selectNote` action. It reads no data from the store.

```
export default connect(
  null, {
    ...actions
  }
)(Note);
```

Edit Note Component

The EditNote component builds a dialog for creating or editing a note.

```
import React, { useState, useEffect } from 'react';
import { connect } from 'react-redux';
import actions from './actions';
import effects from './effects';

function EditNote({
  note, show, category,
  closeCreateNote, deleteNote, saveNote}) {

  const [title, setTitle] = useState('');
  const [content, setContent] = useState('');

  useEffect(() =>{
    setTitle(note.title);
    setContent(note.content);
  }, [note]);

  function createNote(){
    return {
      ...note,
      title,
      content,
      categoryID : category.id
    };
  }

  if(show) {
    return (
      <div className="overlay" >
        <form className="dialog">
          <div className="modal-body">
```

```jsx
        <div className="form-group">
          <input
            type="text"
            value={title}
            className="form-control"
            onChange={e=>setTitle(e.target.value)} />
        </div>
        <div className="form-group">
          <textarea
            rows="4"
            value={content}
            className="form-control"
            onChange={e=>setContent(e.target.value)}>
          </textarea>
        </div>
        </div>
        <div className="modal-footer">
          <button
           type="button"
           className="btn btn-secondary"
           onClick={closeCreateNote}>
             Close
          </button>
          <button
           type="button"
           className="btn btn-danger"
           onClick={() => deleteNote(note.id)}>
             Delete
          </button>
          <button
           type="button"
           className="btn btn-primary"
           onClick={() => saveNote(createNote())}>
             Save
          </button>
        </div>
      </form>
    </div>
  );
} else {
```

```
      return (null);
   }
}
```

The `EditNote` is a stateful component storing the title and the content of a note. The local state is defined using the useState hook.

```
const [title, setTitle] = useState('');
const [content, setContent] = useState('');
```

The state is then used to set the value of text inputs. When the inputs' value changes the state is updated.

```
<form>
  <input
   type="text"
   value={title}
   onChange={e=>setTitle(e.target.value)} />
  <textarea
   value={content}
   onChange={e=>setContent(e.target.value)}>
  </textarea>
</form>
```

The `note` to be edited is taken in props. The useEffect hook is used to detect any change in this data object and update the local state. Changing the local state implies updating the associated form inputs.

```
useEffect(() =>{
  setTitle(note.title);
  setContent(note.content);
}, [note]);
```

The component uses conditional rendering to create the form only when the `show` prop is `true`.

```
if(show) {
  return (
    <div className="overlay" >
      <form>
      </form>
    </div>
  );
} else {
```

```
    return (null);
}
```

It connects to the store to read if the dialog should be shown, the note to be displayed, and the selected category. It also gets the necessary actions and effects.

```
export default connect(
  ({noteDialog, selectedCategory}) => ({
      note: noteDialog.note,
      show: noteDialog.show,
      category: selectedCategory
  }), {
    ...actions,
    ...effects
  }
)(EditNote);
```

The `closeCreateNote` action is dispatched when pressing the close button. The `deleteNote` and `saveNote` effects are dispatched on the delete and save buttons click events.

Category List Component

The `CategoryList` functional component creates an HTML representation of the list of categories. The selected category is shown with a specific background color.

```
import React from 'react';
import { connect } from 'react-redux';

import actions from './actions';
import effects from './effects';

function CategoryList({
  categories,
  selectedCategory,
  deleteCategory,
  selectCategory }) {
  return (
    <ul className="list-group">
      {categories.map(category => {
        return isSelected(category, selectedCategory)
```

```
        ? <li
            key={category.id}
            onClick={() => selectCategory(category)}
            className="list-group-item" >
              <span>{category.name}</span>
              <button
               type="button"
               className="close"
               onClick={() => deleteCategory(category.id)}>
                 <span aria-hidden="true">
                   &times;
                 </span>
              </button>
          </li>
        : <li
            key={category.id}
            onClick={() => selectCategory(category)}
            className="list-group-item">
              <span>{category.name}</span>
          </li>
      })}
    </ul>
  );
}

function isSelected(category, selectedCategory){
  return (category.id === selectedCategory.id)
}
```

The component transforms the categories list into `<li>` elements, each containing a button for selecting that category.

The `map` array method is used to convert each category data object into a `<li>` element.

```
{ categories.map(category =>
    <li
     key={category.id} >
       <span>{category.name}</span>
       <button
        type="button">
       </button>
```

```
    </li>
)}
```

Conditional rendering is utilized to display a simple `<span>` element for the selected category.

```
return isSelected(category, selectedCategory)
  ? <li
    key={category.id}>
      <span>{category.name}</span>
      <button type="button">
        <span aria-hidden="true">
          &times;
        </span>
      </button>
    </li>
  : <li
    key={category.id}>
      <span>{category.name}</span>
    </li>
```

The component needs to connect to the store to read all the categories and the selected one. It also needs access to the `deleteCategory` effect and the `selectCategory` action.

```
export default connect(
  ({categories, selectedCategory}) => ({
      categories,
      selectedCategory
  }), {
    ...actions,
    ...effects
  }
)(CategoryList);
```

New Category Category

The `NewCategory` component adds a new category. It creates a form with a single textbox and a button that appears when the text field is not empty.

```
import React, { useState } from 'react';
import { connect } from 'react-redux';
```

```
import effects from './effects';

function NewCategory({ addCategory }) {
  const [title, setTitle] = useState('');

function addCategoryAndClear(){
    addCategory(title);
    setTitle('');
  }

return (
    <form>
      <div className="form-group">
        <input
          type="text"
          className="form-control"
          value={title}
          onChange={e=>setTitle(e.target.value)} />
      </div>
      { title !== '' &&
        <div>
          <button
            type="button"
            className="btn btn-primary"
            onClick={addCategoryAndClear}>
              Add
          </button>
        </div>
      }
    </form>
  )
}
```

The form component has a local state associated with the text field.

```
const [title, setTitle] = useState('');
```

When the text field is rendered its value property contains the local state value. When the text field value changes, the state is updated and the functional component re-renders.

```
<form>
```

```
  <input
    type="text"
    value={title}
    onChange={e=>setTitle(e.target.value)} />
</form>
```

Stateful components are not pure functions.

The `NewCategory` component uses conditional rendering to display the add button only when the text is not empty.

```
{ title !== '' &&
    <div>
      <button
       type="button">
          Add
      </button>
    </div>
}
```

The component needs to connect to the store in order to dispatch the `addCategory` effect.

```
export default connect(
    null, {
    ...effects
  }
)(NewCategory);
```

App Component

The `App` root component defines the page using the other existing components.

```
import React from 'react';
import CategoryList from './category/CategoryList';
import NewCategory from './category/NewCategory';
import Board from './note/Board';

import 'bootstrap/dist/css/bootstrap.css';
import './App.css'

function App() {
  return (
```

```
  <div className="container">
    <h1>Notes Application</h1>
    <div className="row">
      <div className="col-3">
        <CategoryList />
        <NewCategory />
      </div>
      <div className="col-9">
        <Board  />
      </div>
    </div>
  </div>
);
}

export default App;
```

Recap

In React components can be defined as functions that take state data and transform it into HTML and CSS.

The useState hook makes it possible to define stateful functional components. Form components usually have a local state.

Components connect to the store to read state data and to dispatch actions and effects.

Chapter 12: Functional State Management with Elm

React and Redux embrace functional principles but don't offer full support for writing a practical project using only pure functions.

Next, we are going to look at a purely functional language Elm and how it offers support for building an application using only pure functions.

Elm Architecture

Elm is a functional language used to create web applications. It compiles to JavaScript.

At the core of the Elm Architecture there are three concepts:

- Model, representing all the state of the application
- View, a function transforming the state into HTML
- Update, a function used to update state based on the messages

The Elm application uses the view function to create the HTML displayed on the screen. When the user interacts with the UI, the view sends messages. The Elm runtime intercepts these messages and uses the update function to create the newly updated state. When the state changes, the view is used to create the new HTML and so on.

This cycle repeats as shown in the diagram below.

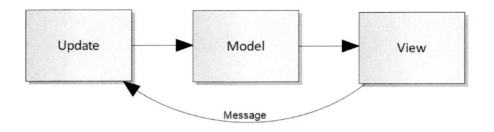

Basically, this is similar to the Redux architecture with different terminology.

Model

The model contains the application state. For the note-taking application, it contains the list of notes, the list of categories, the selected note, the selected category, a boolean indicating if the note dialog should be shown or not.

It is a single tree of immutable data.

It is basically the same as the state concept in Redux.

View

The view is a visual representation of the application model. When a user interacts with the view, it generates messages.

The view is represented by one or several pure functions. These functions take the whole model object or part of it and create HTML elements.

The view functions do not mutate the DOM directly, they just generate markup. The Elm runtime uses them to update the DOM.

Update

The update is a pure function that handles messages by generating a new model.

The update function does not modify the input model. The Elm runtime uses it to generate the new model and apply the change.

It is similar to the reducer concept in Redux.

Commands

In order to handle side-effects, we need to introduce a new concept, commands.

In addition to sending messages on user interaction, Elm can also send commands, like an HTTP request command or a generate a random number command.

In the case of the HTTP command, the Elm runtime intercepts this command, makes the network call, and then triggers a message with the result. For the generate random number command, the Elm runtime intercepts the command, generates the random number, and then triggers a message with the result.

In Elm, we need to create commands describing all kinds of side-effects. The Elm runtime intercepts these commands, runs the side-effects, and then triggers messages with the result. This is the main idea of handling side-effects in Elm using only pure functions.

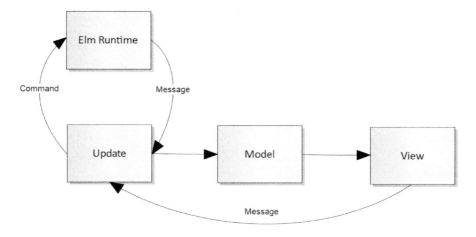

We write the pure functions creating the commands and ELM does the impure part of executing these commands and triggering a message with the result.

Recap

Elm is a functional language compiling to JavaScript that enables us to create a practical application using only pure functions.

The Elm Architecture structures applications into three main parts: the model, the update, and the view.

The model stores all the application data that can change.

The update is a pure function taking the state and a message and returning a new state.

The view is a pure function taking the state and returning the HTML representation of it.

Chapter 13: State Management in Practice with Elm

In this chapter, we will build parts of the note-taking application in a functional style using the Elm purely functional language. The point is to understand the Elm Architecture that allows us to create a practical application using only pure functions.

Start by creating the Elm project.

Navigate to a new folder and create the Elm project by running:

```
elm init
```

Then install the additional required libraries.

```
elm install elm/json
elm install elm/http
```

Start the developing server by running the `elm reactor` command. It starts a server at `http://localhost:8000`. From there we can navigate to any Elm file.

Next, we are going to implement a part of the board page displaying the list of notes.

Records

Note Record

In order to manage notes, we are going to need a `Note` record with all the fields of this entity.

```
type alias Note =
  {
    id: Int,
    title: String,
    content: String,
    categoryID: Int
  }
```

Notes are read from a REST API so we need a function for converting the retrieved JSON into a list of Note records.

The decoder function extracts the field values from a JSON and creates a Note record.

```
import Json.Decode

decoder : Json.Decode.Decoder Note
decoder =
  Json.Decode.map4 Note
    (Json.Decode.field "id" Json.Decode.int)
    (Json.Decode.field "title" Json.Decode.string)
    (Json.Decode.field "content" Json.Decode.string)
    (Json.Decode.field "categoryID" Json.Decode.int)
```

The collectionDecoder creates a list of Note records from a JSON.

```
collectionDecoder : Json.Decode.Decoder (List Note)
collectionDecoder =
  Json.Decode.map identity
    (Json.Decode.list decoder)
```

The Note record, the decoder, and the collectionDecoder functions are public.

```
module Note exposing (Note, decoder, collectionDecoder)
```

Category Record

In order to manage categories, we need a record representing a category.

```
type alias Category =
  {
    id: Int,
    name: String
  }
```

The `decoder` function extracts the field values from a JSON and creates the `Category` record.

```
import Json.Decode

decoder : Json.Decode.Decoder Category
decoder =
  Json.Decode.map2 Category
    (Json.Decode.field "id" Json.Decode.int)
    (Json.Decode.field "name" Json.Decode.string)
```

`collectionDecoder` creates a list of `Category` records from a JSON.

```
collectionDecoder : Json.Decode.Decoder (List Category)
collectionDecoder =
  Json.Decode.map identity
    (Json.Decode.list decoder)
```

The `Category` record, the `decoder`, and the `collectionDecoder` functions will be public.

```
module Category exposing (Category, decoder, collectionDecoder)
```

Model

The model contains the backend data displayed on the screen and the data required for UI functionalities.

The `notes` property stores the list of categories retrieved from the API.

The `categories` property stores the list of categories retrieved from the API.

The `selectedCategory` property keeps the selected category. This is UI only related data that is not retrieved or saved in the backend.

The network request can be in different stages so we start by defining all these states.

```
type RequestState
  = None
  | Pending
  | Success
  | Failure
```

First, we need to create a type with all the Model properties and their types.

```
type alias Model =
  {
    notes: List Note,
    categories: List Category,
    selectedCategory: Category,
    requestState: RequestState,
    error: Maybe String
  }
```

Then we can define the initial value of the Model.

```
initialModel : Model
initialModel =
  {
    notes = [],
    categories = [],
    selectedCategory = { id = 0, name = "" },
    requestState = None,
    error = Nothing
  }
```

Messages

A few messages are required for updating the state. We want also to display a loading message while data is retrieved so for both fetching tasks we need two messages.

FetchNotesStart, FetchNotesEnd mark the start and end of the fetch notes request.

FetchCategoriesStart, FetchCategoriesEnd mark the start and end of the fetch categories request.

SelectCategory is needed for updating the selected category.

```
type Msg
  = FetchNotesStart
  | FetchCategoriesStart
  | FetchNotesEnd (Result Http.Error (List Note))
  | FetchCategoriesEnd (Result Http.Error (List Category))
  | SelectCategory Category
```

Commands

The `fetchNotes` command defines an HTTP Get request to retrieve all the notes. When a response is received from the server the result is transformed into a list of notes using the `Note.collectionDecored` then the `FetchNotesEnd` message with the associated result is sent to Elm runtime.

```
fetchNotes: Cmd Msg
fetchNotes =
  Http.get
    { url = "http://localhost:3001/notes"
    , expect = Http.expectJson
        FetchNotesEnd N.collectionDecoder
    }
```

`fetchCategories` defines a similar command that retrieves the list of categories and dispatches the `FetchCategoriesEnd` message with the result.

```
fetchCategories: Cmd Msg
fetchCategories =
  Http.get
    { url = "http://localhost:3001/categories"
    , expect = Http.expectJson
        FetchCategoriesEnd C.collectionDecoder
    }
```

Update

The update function takes a message and the current model and returns a new model and a command.

When `FetchNotesStart` message is received, the `requestState` model property is set to `Pending` and the `fetchNotes` command is dispatched.

When the `FetchNotesEnd` message is received, the `notes` model property is updated with the new list of notes. No command is triggered.

A similar thing happens when the `FetchCategoriesStart` and `FetchCategoriesEnd` messages are received. This time, the `categories` model property is updated with the new list of categories.

When the `SelectCategory` message is received the `selectedCategory` model property is updated with the new category. No command is triggered.

```
update : Msg -> Model -> (Model, Cmd Msg)
update msg model =
  case msg of
    FetchNotesStart ->
      (
        { model | requestState = Pending },
        fetchNotes
      )

    FetchNotesEnd result ->
      case result of
        Ok notes ->
          (
            { model | requestState = Success, notes = notes },
            Cmd.none
          )

        Err _ ->
          (
            { model | requestState = Failure,
              error = Just "Error"
            },
            Cmd.none
          )

    SelectCategory selectedCategory ->
      (
        { model | selectedCategory = selectedCategory },
        Cmd.none
      )

    FetchCategoriesStart ->
      (
        { model | requestState = Pending },
        fetchCategories
      )

    FetchCategoriesEnd result ->
```

```
case result of
  Ok newList ->
    (
        { model | requestState = Success,
          categories = newList },
        Cmd.none
    )

  Err _ ->
    (
      { model | requestState = Failure,
        error = Just "Error" },
      Cmd.none
    )
```

Views

A few imports are necessary for creating the view functions.

```
import Html exposing
    (Html, button, div, text, br, button, span)
import Html.Events exposing (onClick)
```

The `renderPostItem` function takes a post data object and creates the HTML for it.

```
renderPostItem: Post -> Html Msg
renderPostItem post =
  div [] [
    div [] [ text post.title ],
    div [] [ text post.content ],
    br [] []
  ]
```

The `renderBoard` function takes the whole model and renders the bord with the selected notes.

```
renderBoard: Model -> Html Msg
renderBoard model =
  case model.requestState of
    None ->
      div [] []
```

```
    Pending ->
      div [] [text "Loading..."]

    Success ->
      div [] (
        model.notes
        |> List.filter (\p ->
           p.categoryID == model.selectedCategory.id)
        |> List.map renderPostItem
      )

    Failure ->
      case model.error of
        Just error ->
          span [] [text error]

    Nothing ->
          span [] []
```

Notice how `renderBoard` uses `List.filter` to select only the notes from the selected category. Then it transforms the returned list into HTML using `List.map` and the previous `renderPostItem` pure function.

`renderCategoryItem` takes in a category and the selected category and returns the HTML for it. The selected category is displayed in a <span>element, all the other categories are rendered as buttons.

```
renderCategoryItem: Category -> Category -> Html Msg
renderCategoryItem item selectedItem =
  if item.id == selectedItem.id then
    div [] [
      span [] [text item.name]
    ]
  else
    div [] [
      button
      [ onClick (SelectCategory item)]
      [ text item.name ]
    ]
```

When the category button is clicked the `SelectCategory` message containing the selected category is triggered.

renderCategoryList creates the HTML for a list of categories. It takes the whole model because we also need the current state of the network request. It uses renderCategoryItem to render an item in the list.

```
renderCategoryList: Model -> Html Msg
renderCategoryList model =
  case model.requestState of
    None ->
      div [] []

    Pending ->
      div [] [text "Loading..."]

    Success ->
      div [] (
        model.categories
          |> List.map (\item ->
          renderCategoryItem item model.selectedCategory)
      )

    Failure ->
      case model.error of
        Just error ->
          span [] [text error]

        Nothing ->
          span [] []
```

The view function is the root view function.

It takes the model and creates the HTML for the whole page using all the other view functions.

```
view : Model -> Html Msg
view model =
  div []
    [
      button
        [onClick FetchNotesStart]
        [text "Fetch All Notes"],
      button
        [onClick FetchCategoriesStart]
```

```
        [text "Fetch All Categories"],
        renderCategoryList model,
        renderBoard model
    ]
```

When the fetch notes button is clicked the `FetchNotesStart` message is triggered. The update function receives this message and sends the `fetchNotes` command to the Elm Runtime. The runtime executes the command and triggers the `FetchNotesEnd` with the result.

In a similar way, the fetch categories button triggers the `FetchCategoriesStart` message that starts the `fetchCategories` command which triggers the `FetchCategoriesEnd` with the result.

init

The `init` function describes how to initialize the application. It specifies the program's initial model and a set of commands to be dispatched. When the application starts both `fetchNotes`, `fetchCategories` commands are dispatched to retrieve all the categories and all the notes from the backend.

```
init: (Model, Cmd Msg)
init =
  (initialModel, Cmd.batch [fetchNotes, fetchCategories])
```

Main

The `main` function wires up the init, view, and update functions.

```
main : Program () Model Msg
main =
  Browser.element
    { view = view
    , init = \_ -> init
    , update = update
    , subscriptions = always Sub.none
    }
```

Form State

Next, let's look at a simple example of a module showing a form with a text field and the add button for adding a new category.

Model

The model contains the text of the new category.

```
type alias Model =
  {
    newCategoryTitle : String
  }

initialModel : Model
initialModel =
  { newCategoryTitle = "" }
```

Messages

We need a message for updating the new category title when the user changes the input text.

```
type Msg
  = SetTitle String
```

View

A few imports are required.

```
import Browser
import Html exposing (Html, Attribute, div, input, text)
import Html.Attributes exposing (..)
import Html.Events exposing (onInput)
```

renderAddButton function takes the model and creates the add button inside a <div> element when the title is not empty, otherwise, it just creates an empty <div>.

```
renderAddButton: Model -> Html Msg
renderAddButton model =
  if model.newCategoryTitle /= "" then
    div []
      [button [] [ text "Add"]]
    else
      div [] []
```

The view function takes the model and creates a form displaying the input text field and the add button.

```
view : Model -> Html Msg
view model =
  div []
    [
      div[]
      [
        input
        [ placeholder "New Category",
          value model.title,
          onInput SetTitle ] []
      ],
      div []
        [ text (model.title) ],
      renderAddButton model
    ]
```

Update

The update function takes a message and the current model and returns a new model.

When the SetTitle is received a new model is created with newCategoryTitle property updated with the new value.

```
update : Msg -> Model -> Model
update msg model =
  case msg of
    SetTitle newTitle ->
      { model | newCategoryTitle = newTitle }
```

The update function creates a changed copy of the current model.

Main

The main section wires up the model with the root view and root update functions.

```
main : Program () Model Msg
main =
  Browser.sandbox {
    init = initialModel,
    update = update,
    view = view
```

}

Recap

Records are required for defining the type of data we are working on.

Models keep both the UI and backend related state data.

The root view function can be split into several other pure view functions. The standard HTML elements like buttons, inputs, divs are also pure functions.

The update function returns the new state, but it can also return a new command that will be executed by the runtime.

Chapter 14: Review

We will finish our journey by taking a look back at how state management was handled from an object-oriented approach to a purely functional one.

State

According to Wikipedia, "a system is described as stateful if it is designed to remember preceding events or user interactions; the remembered information is called the state of the system".

In essence, the state is data that is stored and can be changed.

The state was the same in all implementation. It was made of:

- the list of categories
- the list of notes
- the selected category
- the selected note
- the show note edit dialog boolean

Data that doesn't change is just a configuration.

Data taken from the backend and passed from parent to children via props is not state is props.

Object-Oriented with Svelte

Store and state are different concepts. The state is the data value. A store is a behavior object that manages state through methods.

In the note-taking app, the state management was split between three stores managing part of that state:

- the `noteSore`, managing the list of notes
- the `categoryStore`, managing the list of categories

- the `uiStore`, managing all UI related data: the selected category, the selected note, and the show dialog boolean

In Svelte the smart idea is the "derived stored". This solved the problems that appear when splitting the state between several business objects. There is no clear solution for coordinating updates to multiple stores. Our solution was to do that in the component itself. So the component was in charge of transforming the state into HTML using the template but also coordinating state updates.

The overall architecture in this case becomes a layered architecture.

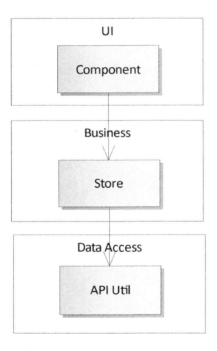

The data travels from the backed API to the stores and from there to the UI components.

Centralized Store with Vue and Vuex

Vuex centralizes all state inside a single store but allows to split the state management between modules. We split the state between two modules:

- the category module, managing the list of categories and the selected category

- the note module, managing the list of notes, the selected note, and the show note dialog boolean

Modules can read the state from other modules. They can also access mutations and actions from other modules. Because of this, the orchestration logic can be extracted out from the component and put into action functions.

Vuex offers a nice set of helpers for connecting components to the store.

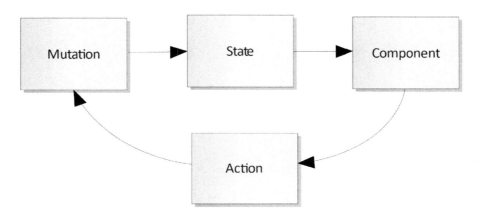

Functional with React and Redux

In a similar way, Redux also centralized all the state in a single store but allows to split the state management between reducers. We grouped these reducers into two features:

- category feature, managing the list of categories and the selected category
- the note feature, managing the list of notes and the note dialog object. The dialog object had two properties, the show dialog boolean and selected note.

React is great at being a view layer. It takes data and turns it into a user interface using functions.

The Redux architecture enables state management using pure functions. Side-effects are encapsulated inside asynchronous actions, which we called "effects". Effects can dispatch other effects, so they may encapsulate orchestration logic.

The state managed by several reducers can be accessed as a single immutable root object.

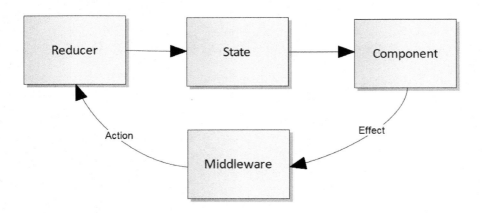

Purely Functional with Elm

The two main concepts in functional programming are immutable data and pure functions.

React has embraced immutability from the start but it didn't really embrace pure functions. React Hooks enabled us to create all kinds of components using functions but it didn't favor pure functions, on the contrary, React hooks are just ways to add side-effects inside the function components.

Redux offers support for side-effects by including the asynchronous actions but it didn't offer support for writing only pure functions.

Elm shows us a way of managing state using only pure functions. This implies the removal of the local state. All state is kept at the application level.

All view functions are pure functions just transforming data into HTML.

The update function is a pure function transforming the current state.

Commands allow handling side-effects using the pure function.
Side-effects are hidden behind the Elm runtime. We create commands describing the side-effects and then the runtime runs these commands and triggers messages with the result. This approach requires that the Elm runtime supports all kinds of side-effects.

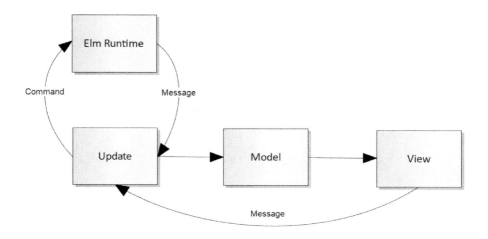

Private vs Public Data

When looking back on how state management is done we notice two approaches.

When data is mutable is also private, meaning that it can only be changed by a specific piece of logic. This is the object-oriented approach where private mutable data is encapsulated behind stores and can be changed using only their public methods.

When data is public is also immutable. It can be read by any part of the code, but it is immutable. So anyone trying to change it has to create a changed copy. This is the functional approach.

The worst option is to have public mutable data. Meaning data that can be changed by any piece of code. Notice that Vuex has limited data changes to the mutation functions only to avoid this scenario.

Final Thoughts

State management implies seeing the UI as a representation of state. Applications store state data and transform it into a visual interface.

In an object-oriented architecture, the state management is split between store objects each managing part of it. Components can read the state by subscribing to the store and can change it by calling the store methods.

In a functional approach, state management implies the use of the unidirectional data flow. The state describes the data of the application at a specific point in time. View functions transform the state into UI elements. Views trigger actions on user interactions. Update functions handle these actions by returning a new state. When the state changes the views using it recreate the UI.

In objected-oriented programming, the state is encapsulated behind store objects. In functional programming, the state is immutable and transformed using pure functions.

What's next?

For a more in-depth look at JavaScript and main functional principles, you may read 'Discover Functional JavaScript'. Here, you will find more on pure functions, immutability, currying, decorators but also ideas on how to make code easier to read. JavaScript brings functional programming to the mainstream and offers a new way of doing object-oriented programming without classes and prototypes.

In the 'Functional Programming in JavaScript' book you will find how to use JavaScript as a functional programming language by disabling the 'this' keyword and enforcing immutable objects with a linter. You will learn how to use statements like 'if' and 'switch' in a functional way, or how to create and use functors and monads. It turns out that JavaScript has everything it needs to be used as a functional language. We just have to remove features from the language.

If you want to learn how to build modern React applications using functional components and functional programming principles, you can consider reading 'Functional React, 2nd Edition'.

Cristian Salcescu

Continue your learning path with 'Functional Architecture with React and Redux' book, and put in practice what you learned by building several applications with an incremental level of complexity.

The functional architecture implies getting the initial state, showing it to the user using the view functions, listening for actions, updating the state based on those actions, and rendering the updated state back to the user again.

Cristian Salcescu

The 'Microblog React Project' book takes a project-based learning approach by engaging you in building a practical application. The reader will learn things on the way by developing different parts of this project. The Microblog application will be built using React with Hooks and libraries like Redux, Redux Thunk, Redux Toolkit, Material UI, or Axios.

Cristian Salcescu

The Composition API provides a new way of managing reactivity. It is made of a set of Reactive API functions plus the facility to register lifecycle hooks. Understand better the reactivity system by building one from scratch and then implement a master-details functionality. Check how to manage state using the Composition API and then use it to implement a central store similar to Vuex.

Enjoy the learning journey!

About the author

Cristian Salcescu is the author of Functional React.

He is a Technical Lead passionate about front-end development and enthusiastic about sharing ideas. He took different roles and participated in all parts of software creation.

Cristian Salcescu is a JavaScript trainer and a writer on Medium.